ADOBE PHOTOSHOP BEGINNER'S GUIDE 2021

ESSENTIAL TECHNIQUES TO MASTERING PHOTOSHOP WITH TIPS AND TRICKS

MICHAEL A. PALMER

Copyright

Printed on acid-free paper.

Printed in the United States of America

Contents

CHAPTER ONE

INTRODUCTION TO PHOTOSHOP 2021 GUIDE

Adobe Photoshop is a raster graphics editor established and published by Adobe Inc. for Windows and macOS. It was initially created in 1988 by Thomas and John Knoll. Since then, the software has become the industry standard not only in raster graphics editing, but in digital art as a whole. The software's name has thus become a generic trademark, leading to its usage as a verb (e.g. "to Photoshop an image", "Photoshopping", and "Photoshop contest") although Adobe discourages such use. Photoshop can be used to edit and create raster images in several supports and layers alpha compositing, masks and numerous color models with RGB, CIELAB, CMYK, duotone and spot color. Photoshop uses its peculiar PSB and PSD file setups to support these characteristics. Adding to raster graphics, Photoshop has restricted abilities to render text or edit and vector graphics (particularly via clipping), along with video and 3D graphics. Its characteristics can be extended by plug-ins; programs advanced and circulate independently of Photoshop running inside it and give new or improved characteristics.

Photoshop's naming structure was originally built on number of version. Nevertheless, in October 2002 (prior to the overview of Creative Suite branding), every version of Photoshop that was new was selected with "CS" plus a number; e.g., the eighth main version of Photoshop was Photoshop CS and the ninth version was Photoshop CS2. Photoshop CS3 via CS6 was likewise distributed in different dual editions: Extended and Standard. By introducing the Innovative Cloud branding in June 2013 (and consecutively, the modification of the "CS" suffix to "CC"), Photoshop's licensing scheme was altered to that of software as a service charge model. In history, Photoshop was pushed with other software like Adobe Fireworks, Adobe ImageReady, Adobe Device Central, Adobe Bridge, and Adobe Camera RAW.

File format

Photoshop files have file extensions that are default as .PSD, signifying "PhotoShop Document." A PSD file saves an image with support for most imaging preferences accessible in Photoshop. They comprise layers with text, masks, alpha channels, transparency and clipping paths, spot colors, and duotone settings. This is different from most file formats (such as .GIF or JPG) that limit content to offer predictable functionality and streamlining. A PSD file has an extreme width and height of 30,000 pixels, and a length boundary of two gigabytes.

Photoshop files however, occasionally have the file extension termed .PSB that signifies "PhotoShop Big" (otherwise called "large document format"). A PSB file spreads the PSD file format, accumulating the extreme width and height to 300,000 pixels and the length border to maybe 4 gigabytes. The limit of the dimension was actually selected indiscriminately by Adobe, not centered on computer arithmetic limitations (it is not near a control of two, since is 30,000) but then for stress-free software testing, PSB and PSD designs are documented.

Because Photoshop is well-known, PSD files are generally used and backed up to some level by various competing software, which includes Open-Source/Free Software like GIMP. The .PSD file format can as well be exported to and from Adobe's other applications like Adobe Premiere Pro, Adobe Illustrator and After Effects.

How to Disable Photoshop Home Screen

- Open 'Photoshop'

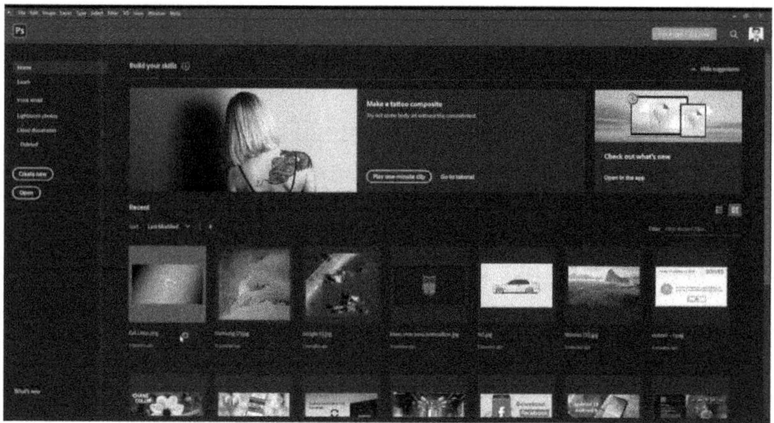

- Click 'Edit' at the top of the window

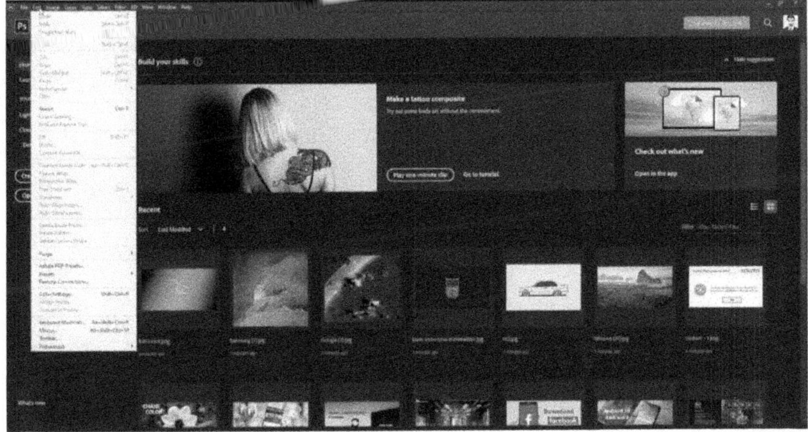

- Select the 'Preferences' at the bottom of the pop-up menu

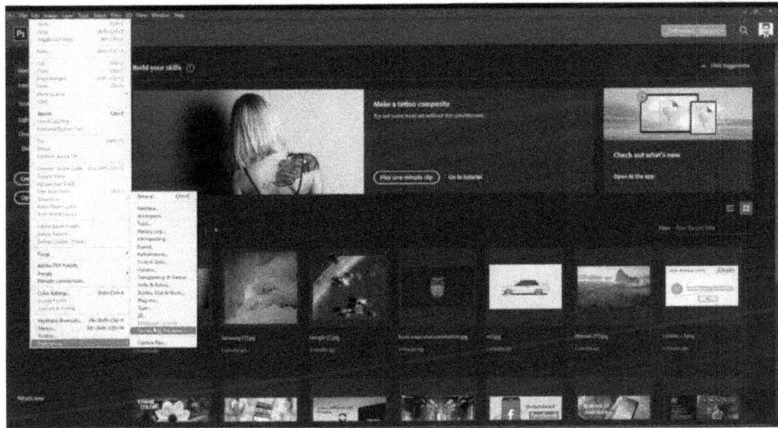

- Select the 'General' option

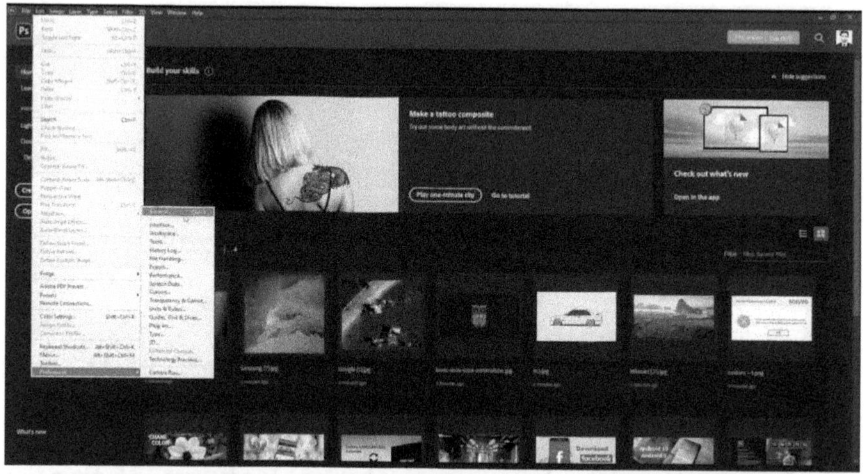

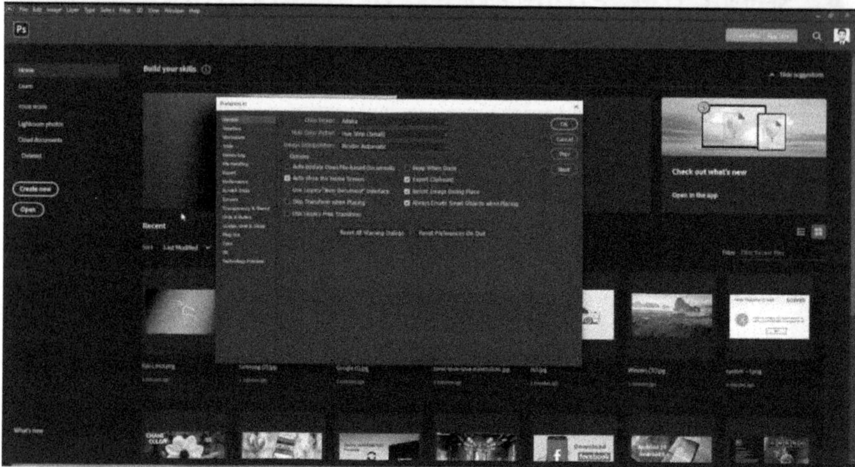

Note: You can alternatively open this menu using the shortcut on your keyboard 'Ctrl + k'

- Then check the box to the left of auto show the Home Screen
- And click the 'ok' button at the top right of the window

- The subsequent time you launch Photoshop, it would open without the home screen

Note: You can always come back to this menu later if you would like to restart the home screen

How to Create a New Document from the Home Screen

- Again, the Photoshop home screen offers an easy and a faster access to create new documents.
- Simply tap 'File' and click "New" under the popup menu

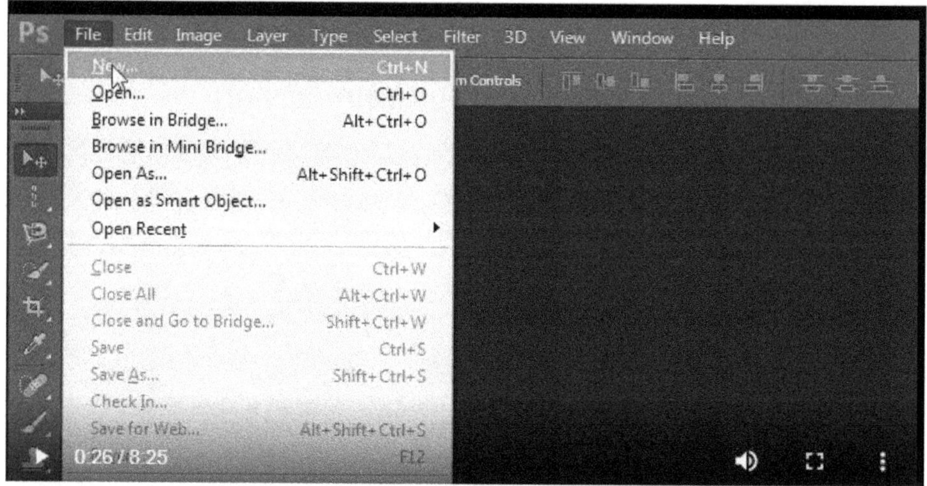

- Then, you'll be given a "New Document" window. However, do you know that there are two separate types of "New Document" windows?
- The New Document window originates from 2 flavors: New and Legacy.
- The "legacy" window was the automatic interface for users of Photoshop for some time before the invention of a "New Document" window with numerous options which are more visual.

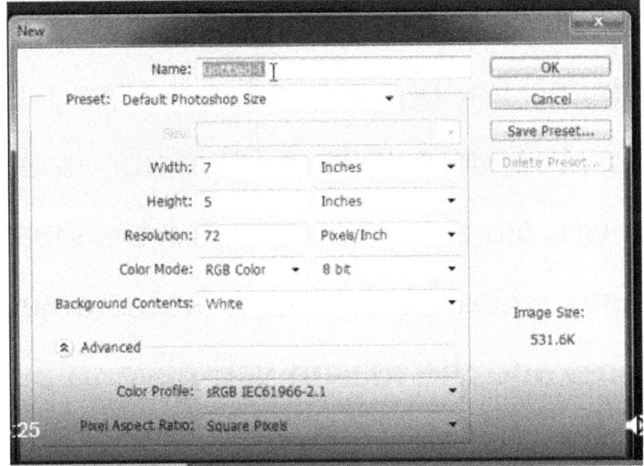

How to create a new document with the "legacy" window...

- Name – Give your document a name.
- Document type – There's a lot to select from.
- If you are sure of the particular size required, then simply input the dimensions through the height and width fields. Or better still select from any of the pre-made template options not neglecting to set the resolution. 72 for web documents or 300 for print. Including the idea of setting the size considering the inches, pixels etc..
- To adjust the option, tap the drop-down menu at the right of the Height and Width.

- Color Mode? Except you intend to create a document for printing on a printing press, that means the default of RGB Color is suitable for now. Oh, did I mention that 8 bit is ideal too.
- Pending when you become accustomed to these features and the reason you have to adjust them, leave them on the defaults.
- If you wish, you can store the setup for the new document as a preset. Better if you wish to use the same settings for upcoming projects.
- Tap on "Save Preset," give it a name and tap "Ok."
- At this moment, tap on "OK." Your home screen shows and your new document are opened in your Photoshop workspace.

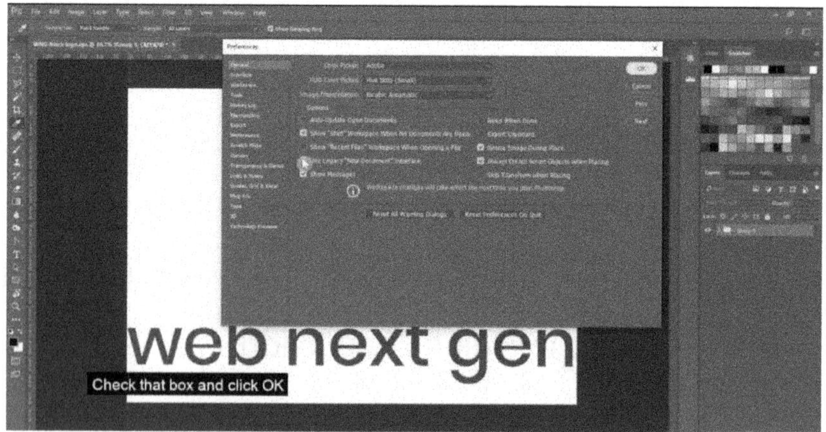

How to create a new document with the "new" window...

Anyway, the features are somehow similar to the legacy window. Though, it's more visual.

Just as the legacy, you can select from pre-made templates (types of document), save presets, and automatically enter the dimensions of your new document.

The Photoshop home screen provides a quicker and easier way to view previous projects, open and continue working on.

How to Open Images from the Home Screen

- The Photoshop home screen offers a quicker and easier way of opening images. At the left side of your home screen, tap on 'File' then 'Open' to see a dialogue box.
- From there, a window will be opened by the operating system that will enable the navigation of the file you intend to open.
- Locate the image and tap "open" (below the right side of the new window). Note that you can as

well drag the image to the Photoshop home screen.

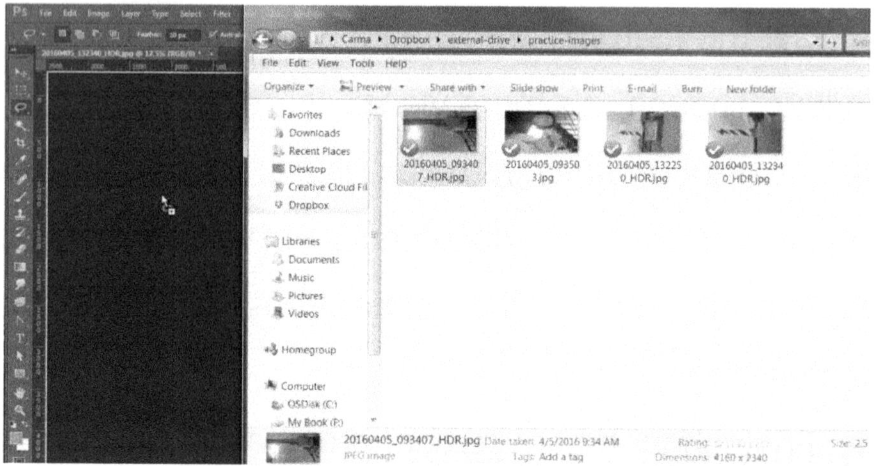

- An additional technique of opening an image, from your home screen, is to just tap on a list of thumbnails in the "Recent" section.

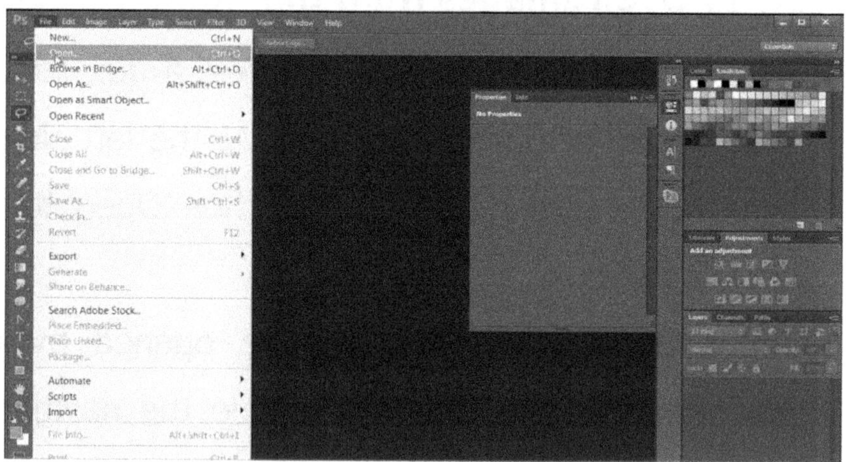

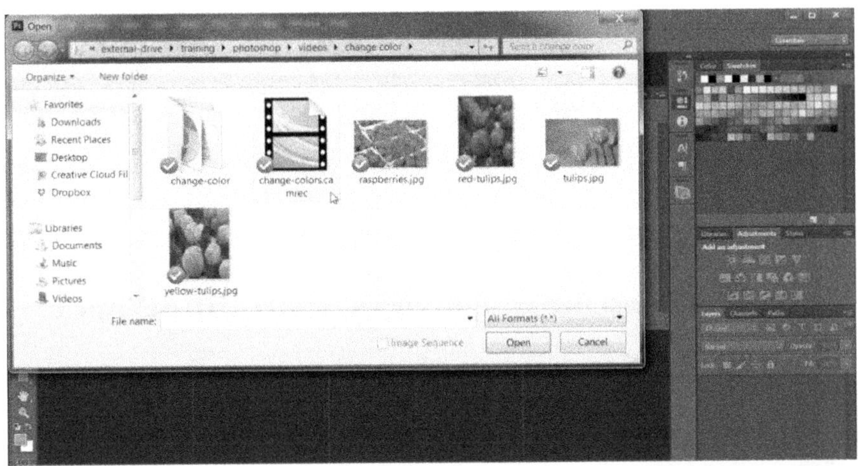

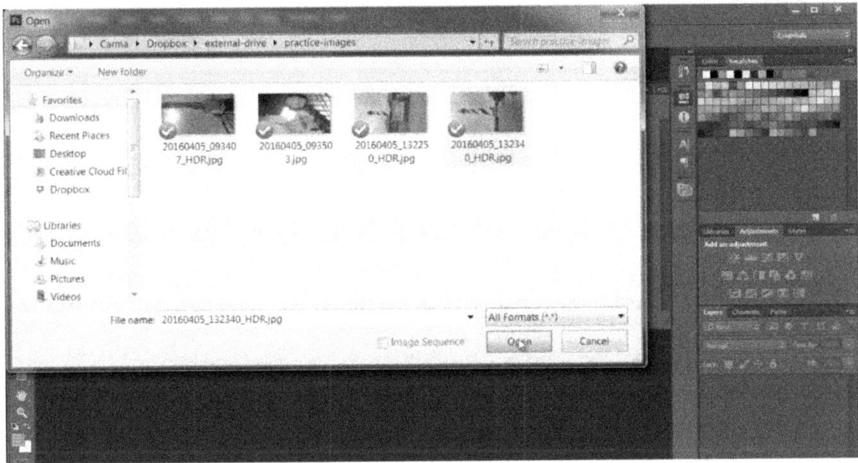

How to Filter Your Home Screen for Particular Files

- At the center of the Photoshop home screen interface comprises all the "recent" files.
- The center of the Photoshop home screen interface comprises of all your "recent" files.

- The view of these files is present in 2 flavors: List and Thumbnails.

Views

- In my point of view, Thumbnails are a preferable method because it's very easy to regulate the particular file you want, by viewing it vs. analyzing a file name.
- An additional benefit of the "list" vs. the "thumbnail" is the data given beneath each thumbnail. You will see the file name together with the duration of time that the file was opened.
- The list offers this info and the particular file size. Therefore, to me, without a thumbnail, I might choose the right file.
- I usually work on various versions of files and will give the files a name accordingly: that is, 1st Edition, 2nd Edition, etc.
- You can easily tell the version of a file you intend to work on by viewing it vs. only the name of the file. But you will have to choose the method that works better for you.

Sort

- You also have the option of organizing your "Recent" files according to the "Sort" options you choose. The automatic choice is to sort the files by "Last Opened"
- It then means your list or your thumbnails will be arranged using the files you recently worked on via the oldest file.
- However, it can be adjusted from oldest to newest by tapping on the (teeny tiny) arrow at the right of the menu.
- Files can also be sorted by Name, Kind (a file type), and Size.

Sort by Filter

- When you intend to take your recent file to a few, simply use the "Filter option at the right.
- Thought it doesn't actually work as I envisaged it would. It's somehow limited since there are only 20 most recent files you opened on the list.
- That means, you are filtering the 20 files down to a certain few. How it works for you will determine

how you will name your files. For instance, if I input a certain number, e.g. number 3…

- You will then find out that there are numerous files with the #3 added in the name.
- When I am sure of the particular file name (or something similar to it), as 366, that means, it will go back to only 1 image.

Search

- An alternative option to filter is done through the 'Search' option. An additional option for filtering can be completed using the Search option. In the top right of the interface, you'll discover a magnifying glass. Tap on it.
- Now, when you input similar number as before, 3. Similar 4 "Currently Opened" files are shown as before. Nevertheless, there is now a new panel of photos beneath them named: Adobe Stock.
- Therefore, Adobe has suitably included photos (from the stock agency) to the home screen believing that you will find a photo that can be used for your project.

- Now, enter the word "landscape" and look for pictures with the keyword.
- At this time, I do not have a listed currently opened file. Then, I currently have a picture from my Lightroom CC cloud account recorded above.

CHAPTER TWO

THE DOCUMENT SETUP

Step 1:

- Go to 'File' and click 'new'
- Duplicate the Background of the layer
- Begin by creating a copy of an image. In the Layers panel, tap on the layer's Background and take it to the New Layer icon: A copy will display at the top of the original.
- Then click twice on the Background name copy to highlight it:
- Double-click the layer's name to adjust it
- And adjusting a layer's name to 3D. Tap 'Enter' (Win) / 'Return' (Mac) to agree to it

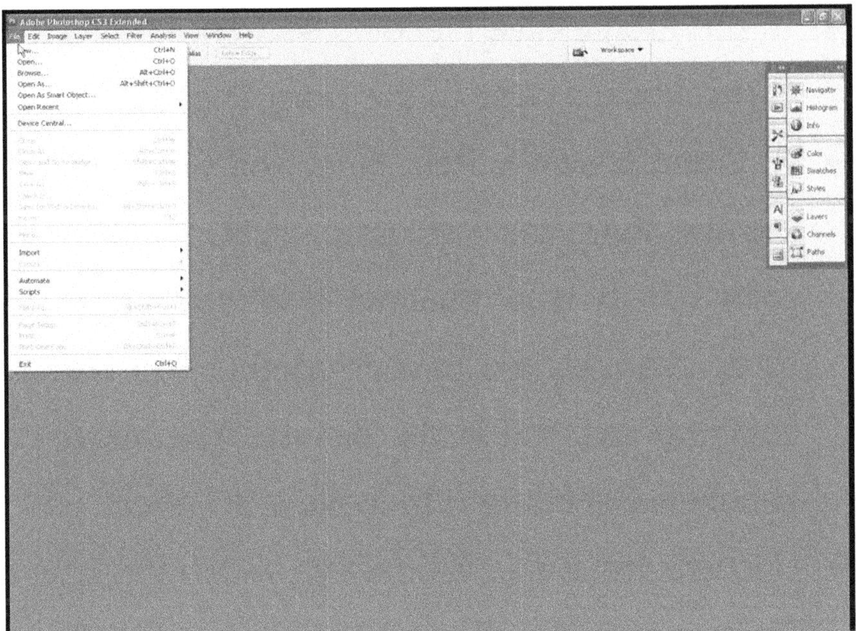

Step 2:

- Open a Layer Style dialog box
- With the active 3D layer, tap the fx icon below the Layers panel:
- Click on the layer's effect icon in the Photoshop Layers panel
- And select Blending options above the list

Step 3:

- Turn off the Blue and Green color channels
- Photoshop launches a Layer Style dialog box, using the Blending Options at the center column.

- In the Progressive Blending section, find R, B and G checkboxes close to the word Channels:
- R, B and G signify Red, Blue, and Green and they are the three main colors of light. Every primary color has its color channel in Photoshop, and the three channels are mixed together to make each color we can find in the picture. The above color channels will be used to make a 3D effect.
- Uncheck the B and G boxes to switch the Blue and Green channels off, and then leave the Red (R) channel turned on. And tap 'OK' to close the Style Layer dialog box:
- To view what's occurred, go back to the Layers panel and hide the layer's Background by tapping its visibility icon:
- With just a 3D layer visibility, and with the Blue and Green channels switched off, the image would display in red:
- Turn the Background layer back on by tapping the empty box where the visibility icon normally appears:

The image will then return to full color

Step 4:

- Choose the 'Move' Tool
- All that needs to be done now is to offset the photo on the 3D layer to bring it out of it's alignment with the original image under it
- To effect this, just choose the 'Move' tool from your Toolbar
- To perform that, first select the Move Tool from the Toolbar:

Step 5:

- Take the picture to your left
- By selecting the 3D layer in the Layers panel, use your left arrow key on the keyboard to take the picture on the layer to the left. As the image is moving, a red outline displays through one side of every object in the image. And since cyan is the conflicting color of red, a cyan outline (the other color in those old red and blue 3D glasses) displays through the other side, making our retro 3D effect.

- The more you push the image on the 3D layer, the heavier the red and cyan outlines would display. So change the effect till you're satisfied with the outcome.
- Shapes and text of different styles, effects and color can be added to an image. The Vertical and Horizontal Type of tools to make and edit text can be used. You can also make single-line photograph text or text.

About text

- Use the Vertical Type and Horizontal Type tools to form and edit text.
- For Horizontal type: Click 'Help' then 'About Photoshop'
- Click the 'T' icon below the left corner of the page to select the horizontal format and type in the text you wish to appear in horizontal format
- Uncheck the check sign close to 3D at the top menu of your screen

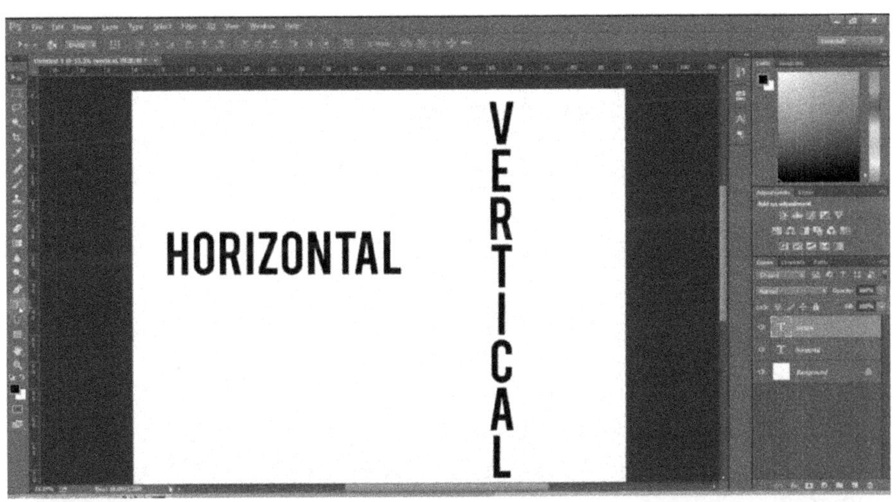

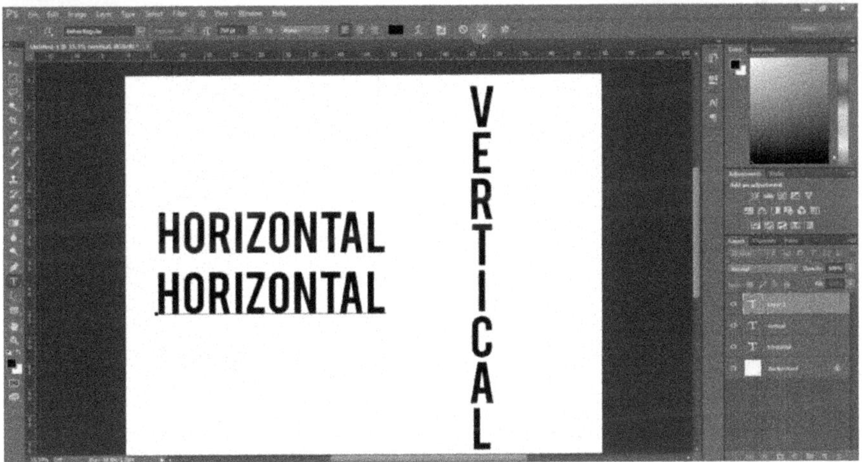

- The recent text you input is entered in another text layer. Paragraph text or single-line text can be created. Every line of a particular line text you input is independent – the distance of a line increases and decreases as you edit it, but doesn't wrap to another line. In forming a new line of text, tap 'Enter.'

- Paragraph text wraps inside the paragraph boundaries you identified.
- For Vertical format: Head into the icon 'T' and select the vertical format and click on the page to type in what you intend to present in a vertical format.

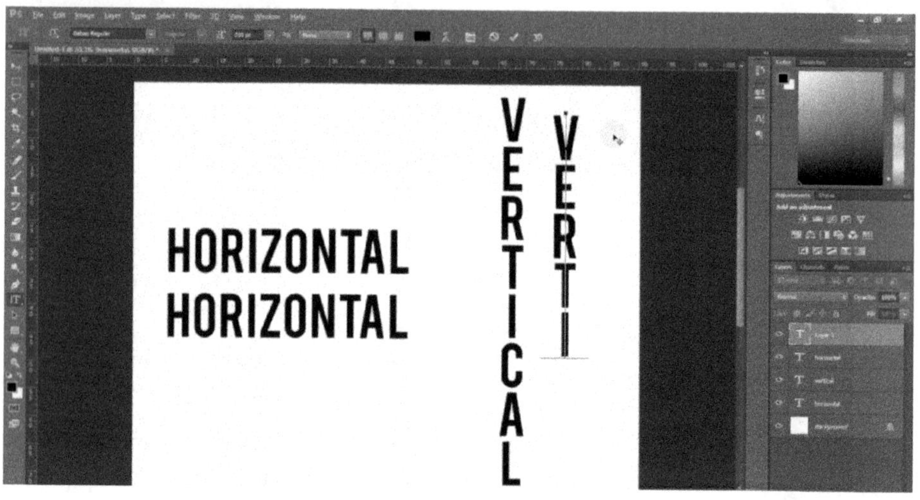

Note: The text can be adjusted to whatever position you need it by dragging it and the horizontal text can be changed to a vertical text vice versa.

- If you include text to any image that is in indexed color mode, Photoshop Elements does not make a new text layer. The text layer you entered displays as masked text.

- From your toolbar, choose the Vertical Type tool and the Horizontal Type tool.

Do any of the following:

- To make a single line of text, tap on the image to configure an insertion point for the type.
- To make paragraph text, drag a rectangle to make a textbox for the type.
- The minor line over the I-beam signifies the type baseline location. For horizontal type, the baseline signifies the line that the type rests; for the vertical type, the baseline signifies the middle axis of your type characters.
- (Optional) Choose type options, e.g. style, font, color and size, in your tool options bar.
- Input the characters you prefer. If a textbox is not created, tap 'Enter' to make a new line.
- The text displays in its layer. To see the layers, in the Expert mode, click 'F11.'

How to use Text on Shape tool

- You can include text to shapes accessible in the Text on Shape tool.

- Choose the Text on Shape tool. To quickly adjust the present text tool, tap Option and tap the current tool.
- From the shapes available, choose the shape that you wish to add text. Drag your cursor on the photo to create the shape.
- To include text to the image, hover your mouse through the path till your cursor icon turns to show text mode. Tap the point to include text.
- Adjust text just as you adjust normal text.
- Tap and input text
- When you have included text, tap 'Commit.' For various shapes the text has to be inscribed inside. The text can be moved round the path or by outside/inside by holding Cmd when tapping and dragging your mouse (The text displays in a small arrow). You can drag your cursor through a particular area; the text path is accessible outside/inside an area.

How to use the Text on Selection tool

- Include text on the outline of a track made from a choice. When a commitment is selected, the selection transforms to a path which you can input text.
- Choose the text on the Selection tool. To swiftly adjust the present text tool, press Option and tap the present tool.

2. Put your cursor on the shape in the image and drag your cursor till when you get your preferred selection. The size of the selection can be adjusted with the Offset slider.

- Create selection
- If the selection is confirmed, it will be converted to a path.

3. To include text to an image, take your mouse through the path and if the cursor icon changes to portray text mode. Tap the point to include text.

- Include text
- When you have added text, you can now change it like a regular text.

4. When you are done adding text, tap 'Commit' and 'Cancel' to begin the workflow over.

- Text can be used on Custom Path tool
- Text can be drawn and added along the custom path
- Choose the Text on Custom Path tool. To change the present text tool, tap 'Option' and tap the current tool.
- Draw a custom path over the image. You can commit/cancel the drawn path to redraw from the tool options bar.
- To redraw or improve the path, tap Modify in the tool options bar. Use the nodes displaying on the path to adjust it.
- When you are done creating the path, tap your mouse at whichever point along the path to include text. Adjust text similar to the way that you have adjusted normal text.
- Include text
- When you have added text, tap the 'Commit.'

Create and use masked type

- The Horizontal Type Mask tool and Vertical Type Mask tool make a selection in the shape of text. Text borders selection can be exciting when cutting text out of an image to display the background, or pasting the text selected into a new image. Experiment with various options to personalize your compositions and images.
- When using an Expert mode, choose the layer that you wish the selection should display. For effective results, ensure you don't create a type selection border around a text layer.
- Tap on the 'T' icon at the left side of your toolbar.
- Then choose the Horizontal Type Mask or the Vertical Type Mask tool.

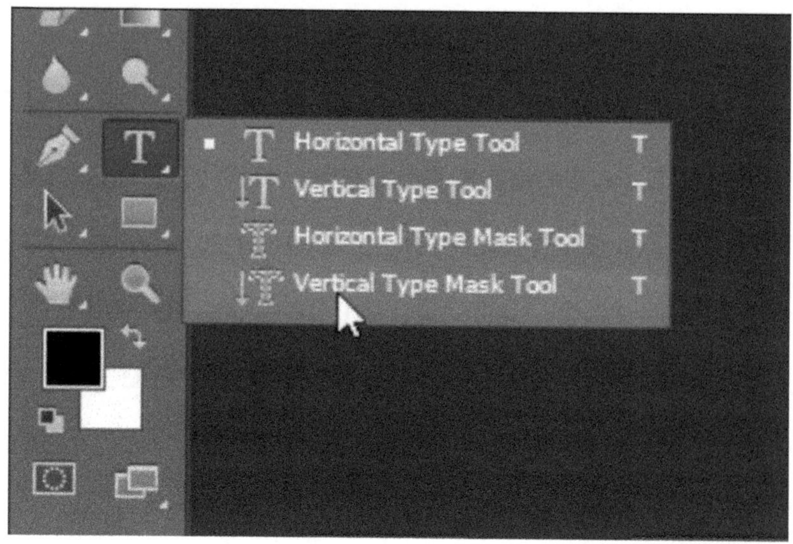

- Tap on the image and it would adjust the color to filter
- Tap on the 'T' icon at the top menu bar and select your preferred Text Point e.g. 60pt at the top menu bar

- Tap on the background of the image and input your text.

- Click on the √ icon at the top right menu and it would display (commit any current edits) to change the background back to its original form

- Hit on Ctrl + J to create another layer that would display only the write-up

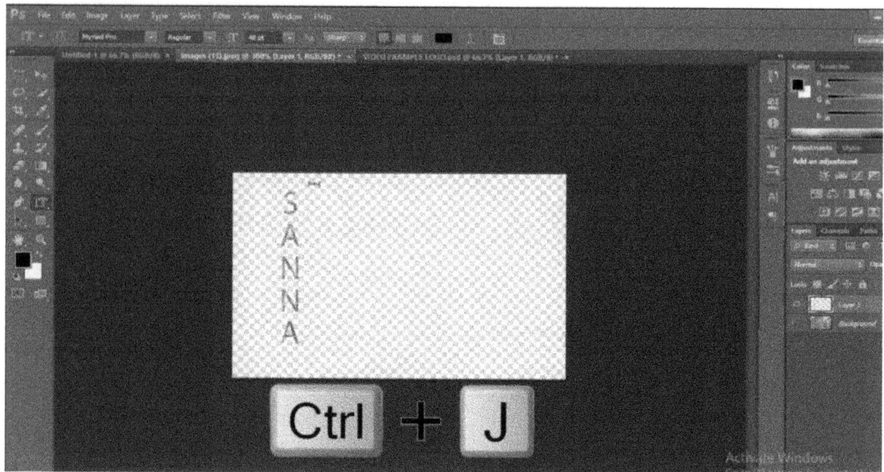

- Right-click on layer 1 to select blending options from the popup menu and it would display layer style options
- Select 'Bevel and Emboss' by checking the box and clicking on it

- Increase the 'Depth' option according to how you want it and either change the direction to up or down
- Also click and drag to increase or decrease the size and soften
- Select 'Stroke' from the left side of the layer style
- Select the preferred size, for instance '1'
- Double click on the color and select any color of your choice by clicking on it

- You can give it a shadow by tapping on 'Drop Shadow' and increasing the distance.

Note: You can also click to increase the spread and size

- Adjust the quality when you tap on 'Quality' and tap the contour box to select any one you like
- Click on the text on your image to move it to a different place if you want
- Tap 'Ctrl + T' and click on the edges of the text and drag it to increase it

CHAPTER THREE

CREATE A SHAPE

You can study how shapes can be created on your canvas and engage the Live-Shape properties to relate with the shapes.

Photoshop has been designed in such a way that it has the feature of drawing and editing vector shapes at ease.

If you can follow these prompt steps in creating shapes in Photoshop:

- Choose a shape tool
- From your toolbar, tap and hold a Shape tool group icon to take out the numerous options of the shape tool — Rounded Rectangle, Rectangle, Ellipse, Polygon, Triangle, Custom Shape and Line. Choose a tool for the shape you intend to draw.
- In options for shape tool bar, the following can be configured:

Mode: Configure a style for the Shape tool — Path, Shape, and Pixels.

Fill: Select a color to fill your desired shape.

Stroke: Select a color, type of the shape stroke and width.

Path operations: Path operations can be used to configure the extent to which your shapes would relate with each other.

W&H: Automatically configure the height and width of the shape.

Path alignment: Path alignment can be used in aligning and distributing the components of your shape.

Path arrangement: Path arrangement can be used to configure the stacking order of shapes you have created.

Other shape and path options: Tap on the gear icon to get other path options and shape to set features like color and width of the on-screen show of your path, and limited options when you are drawing shapes.

Shape tool bar options

Draw a shape

- Tap on the canvas and drag through the shape tool you have selected to draw a shape. It forms a new shape layer automatically in the Layers panel.
- Tap and hold the Shift key when you are drawing to create your shapes more relational.
- Using the shape layer of your choice, the Move tool can be used to move the shape from place to place and relocate the canvas.
- To scale easily, change, or alternate the shape, select 'Edit' then 'Free Transform' or tap 'Control + T (Win)' / 'Command + T (Mac).'

Editing shape properties

- The shape properties can be directly edited easily using the on-canvas control or opening Live Shape Properties below the Properties panel. The On-canvas controls enable you to interact with the shapes more.

- Your shapes properties can be easily edited directly using the on-canvas controls or accessing Live Shape Properties below the Properties panel. The On-canvas controls make your interaction with shapes in a natural way.
- The rounding controls and on-canvas transform can be used to modify the look of a shape. The keyboard transformers will function in a similar technique for on-canvas controls as they also function in the Transform tool in Photoshop.
- The radius of every angle of the shape can be adjusted at a time or press and hold the 'Alt (Win)' or 'Option (Mac)' as you drag to adjust the radius of a particular angle. For triangular shapes, every angle will be changed even when you drag a particular one. Simply rotate a shape with the on-canvas switch handle displaying as you drift through the canvas shape.
- Tap the reset icon in the properties panel for resetting the whole modifications at whichever time.

Live Shapes

- Draw any shape while you use the on-canvas controls to edit properties of shape easily.
- When a shape has been drawn, you can tap anyplace on the canvas to display a "Create Shape" popup dialog, including changing the shape parameters.

Stroke and Fill shapes

- You can follow these prompt steps to stroke and fill shapes:
- On a Layers panel, choose the layer shape you wish to stroke or fill.
- Perform any of the options below to set a shape stroke or fill type:
- Choose a shape tool (tap U) from your toolbar. In your tool bar options, choose Stroke or Fill.
- In the Properties panel, tap the stroke or fill type option.
- A pop-up menu would display, select a stroke or fill option – Gradient, Solid Color or Pattern.

Solid Color: Strokes or Fills a layer shape with the present foreground color. The color presets or the color picker can be used to choose another color.

Gradient: Select a gradient preset or tap on the gradient in viewing the Gradient Editor dialog. Configure other gradient options:

- Angle identifies the angle that the gradient is rightly applied.
- Reverse tosses the alignment of the gradient colors.
- Style identifies the shape of the gradient.
- Scale adjusts the magnitude of the gradient.
- When you align with the layer using the bounding box of the layer in estimating the gradient file, the image window can be dragged in to change the middle of the gradient.

Pattern: Select any pattern from a displayed menu and configure further pattern options:

- Angle identifies the position in which a pattern is used. Configure the angle picker at a particular degree or physically input an angle rate to rotate the pattern of the preferred angle.

- Scale adjusts the size of a pattern. Input a value or drag a slider.

Draw a custom shape

- Custom shapes can be drawn with the use of shapes from a Custom shape displayed panel or save a path.
- Choose your Custom Shape tool from the shape tools in your toolbar.
- To show the whole custom shapes that originated with Photoshop, tap the gear icon at the right of the Custom Shape Selector in the Shape tool options bar. Then, you will find available list of accessible shapes. Choose a custom shape you prefer.
- If you can't locate a preferred shape, tap the gear icon on the Custom Shape selector panel and choose Import Shapes options to import a preferred shape from your files saved. You can as

well make and store a custom shape in your library.

- Click 'File' at the left top side of your menu bar and click 'New'

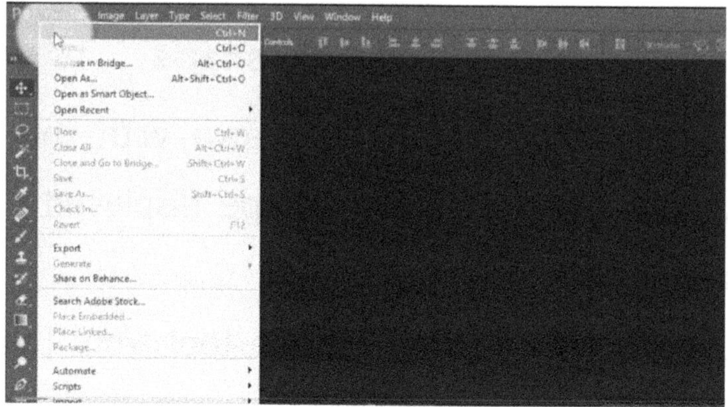

- Set height and weight to '10' and resolution to '300'

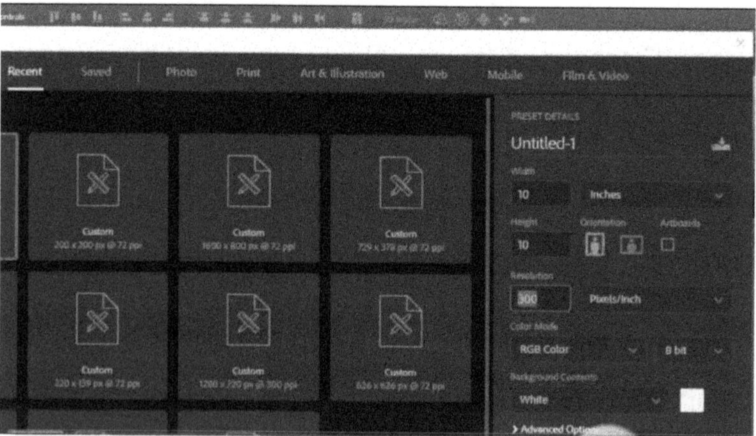

- Now create any shape you wish to create using different tools

- Tap on the background of your working environment and drag to create the shape

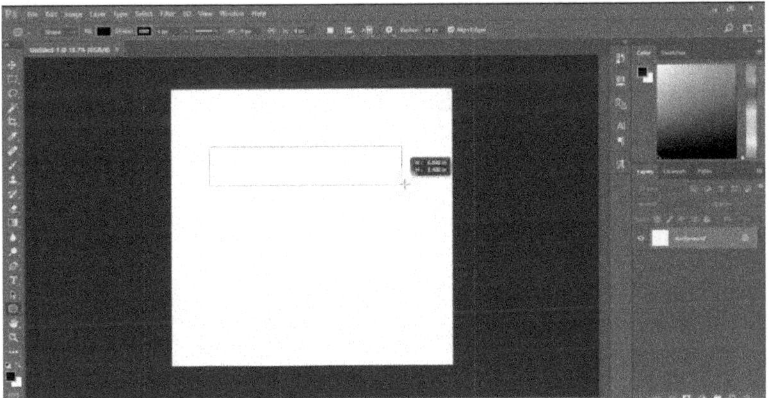

- Choose the preferred properties from your popup menu and you can as well change the size of the pixel to modify the shape form

- Click on [icon] and tap on the shape to drag to any position of your choice
- Tap and drag the rounded rectangle layer to duplicate the layer
- Right click on the shape and drag to duplicate it
- After duplicating, click and drag to whatever position you want

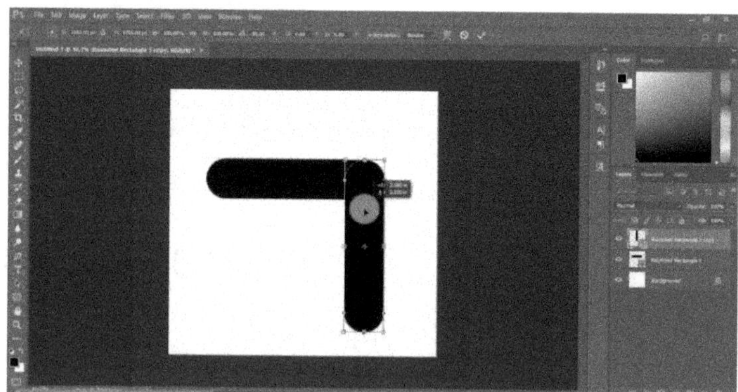

- Adjust the opacity

- Once you are done creating shape, merge your shape without the background by right clicking on the layer and click 'merge shape' on the popup menu
- Right click on the layer and click on 'Rasterize layer' from your popup menu
- Press 'Ctrl' on your keyboard and click the shape layer to make a selection
- Select any of the selection tool, right click and choose 'work path'
- Adjust the tolerance level and click 'ok'

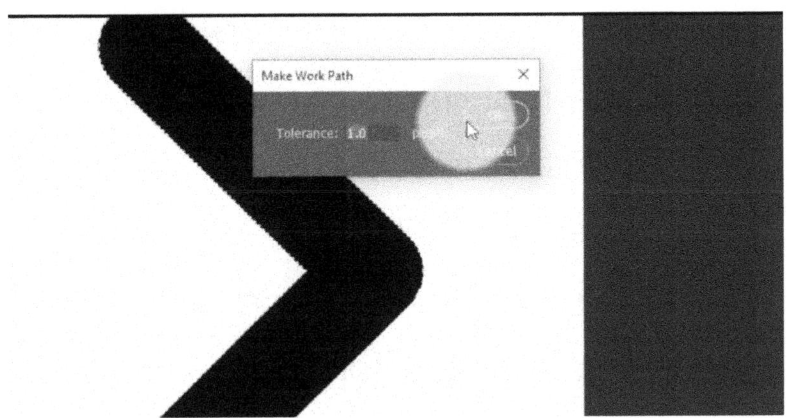

- Select 'pen' tool, right click on the background and choose 'define custom shape'

- Give a name to your shape and press enter
- Click on [icon] to enable you drag the shape to whatever position you desire
- Click [icon] and right click on the background to select 'make work path' then click 'ok'
- Click [icon] and right click the background to select 'define custom shape' to give it a name
- Click on [icon] and click outside the background to make the shape invisible
- Click [icon] to select 'custom shape tool'
- Select shapes at the top menu and choose the desired shape, then tap the shapes again

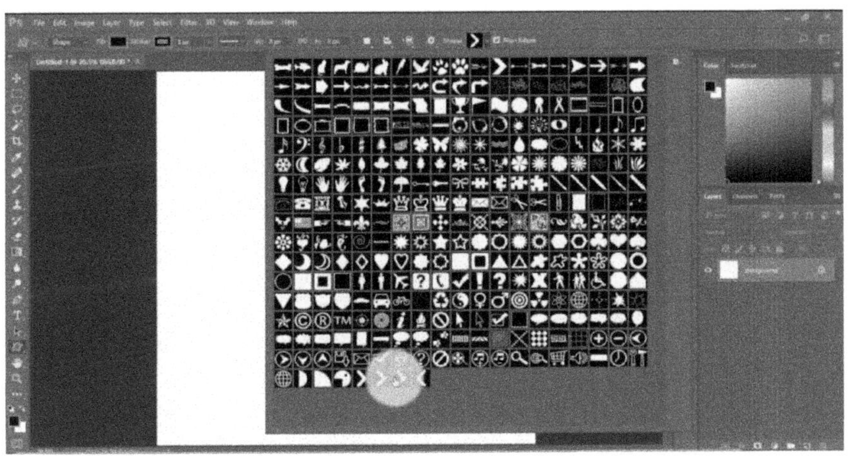

- Click on the background and drag your cursor to create the shape
- Click on the layer at the left and choose the preferred color from your color picker menu and tap 'ok'

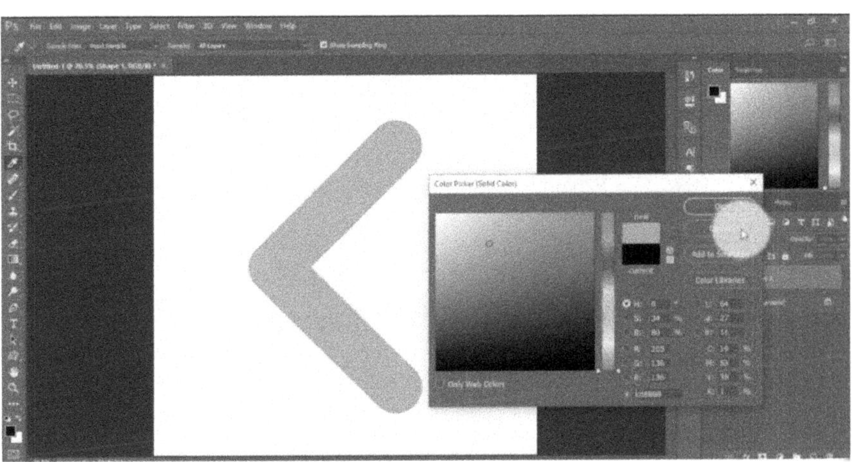

Create a Curve shape

- Click 'File' and tap 'New'

- Click on the background and edit the name, preset, width, heights etc. and click 'ok'

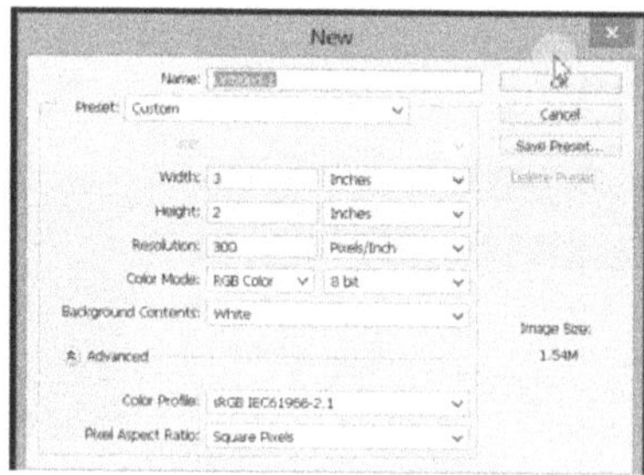

- Select 'pen' tool
- Put your mouse at the various strategic points to draw a rectangular shape

- Click and select 'add anchor point tool'

Custom shape picker

- Tap and drag wherever you like in the canvas to create a custom shape.

Save a path or shape as a custom shape

- In a Paths panel, choose a path—maybe a vector mask for a shape layer, a work path, or a saved path.
- Select 'Edit' then 'Define Custom Shape', and input a title for the different custom shape in the dialog box Shape name. The new shape displays on the Shape display panel in the options bar.
- For you to save a new custom shape as a portion of a new library, choose "Save Shapes" from the displayed panel menu.

Draw a star shape using the Polygon tool

A simple shape we used in drawing as kids was a five-corner star shape.

Following the 3 prompt steps below to draw a star shape with the Polygon shape tool:

- From your toolbar, tap and hold your shape tool group icon to show the concealed shape tool options. Choose the Polygon tool.
- Drag on the canvas to draw a polygon.
- Click wherever you like on the canvas to show the 'Create Polygon' dialog and configure the following features:

Number of Sides: Manually input the number of sides you would prefer the polygon to have. For instance, configure the number of sides to 5 if you wish to draw a 5-angled star shape.

Symmetric: Choose the checkbox to keep symmetry in your polygon.

Width & Height: Manually configure the height and width of the polygon.

Corner Radius: Manually configure a radius to get a rounded corner for the polygon.

Smooth Star Indents: Choose the checkbox to end the star indents.

Star Ratio: Change the Star Ratio percentage to have the best star shape.

From Center: Choose the checkbox to modify the star-shape from the middle.

Transform freely

The Free Transform feature allows you to apply transformations (scale, rotate, skew, perspective and distort) in a constant operation. You can as well apply a warp transformation. Rather than selecting various commands, you can just hold down a particular key on your keyboard to change between transformation types.

Note: When a shape is being transformed or the whole path, the Transform feature changes to the Transform Path command. When transforming numerous path segments (but not the whole path), the Transform tool turns out to be the Transform Points command.

Choose what you intend to transform.

Do any of the following:

- Select 'Edit' then 'Free Transform.'
- When transforming a pixel-based layer, selection or selection border, select the 'Move tool' and choose Display Transform Controls in the bar options.
- When transforming a path or a vector shape, choose the Path Selection tool and choose Display Transform Controls in the options bar.

Do any of the following or more:

- To scale by dragging, do any of the following:
- When the 'Maintain Aspect Ratio' button (Link icon) is ON in your Options bar, drag a corner handle to proportionally scale the layer.
- When the 'Maintain Aspect Ratio' button (Link icon) is OFF in your Options bar, drag a corner handle to non-proportionally scale the layer.
- Press and hold the 'Shift' key when transforming to toggle amid proportional and non-proportional scaling character.

- To numerically scale, input percentages in the Height and Width text boxes in your options bar. Tap the Link icon to keep the aspect ratio.
- To drag when rotating, move your pointer outside the bounding border (it turns to a curved and two-sided arrow) then drag. Tap Shift to limit the rotation to 15^0 increases.
- To numerically rotate, input degrees in the rotation text box in your options bar.
- To relatively distort to the midpoint of the bounding border, tap Alt (Windows) or Option (MacOS) while dragging a handle.
- To freely distort, tap 'Ctrl (Windows)' or 'Command (Mac OS)', and drag a handle.
- To skew, tap 'Ctrl + Shift (Windows)' or 'Command + Shift (Mac OS)', and drag a side handle. If you position through a side handle, your pointer changes to a white arrowhead with a slight double arrow.

- To numerically skew, input degrees in the V (Vertical skew) and H (Horizontal skew) text boxes in your options bar.
- To apply viewpoint, tap 'Ctrl + Alt + Shift (Windows)' or 'Command + Option + Shift (Mac OS), and drag a corner handle. If you positioned it through a corner handle, the pointer changes to gray arrowhead.
- To warp, tap the 'Switch' Between 'Free Transform' and 'Warp Modes' button in your options bar. Drag the control points to handle the shape of the item or select a warp form from the Warp displayed menu in your options bar. After selecting from your Warp displayed menu, a square handle is accessible for changing the shape of the warp.
- To adjust the reference point, tap a square on the reference point locator in your options bar.
- In moving an item, input values for a different place of the reference in the Y (vertical position) and X (horizontal position) text boxes in your

options bar. Tap the 'Relative Positioning' button to identify the present location while relating to the recent position.

Note:

For you to undo the previous handle changes, select 'Edit' then 'Undo.'

Do any of the following function to commit a transformation:

- Choose a new tool.
- Tap a layer in your Layers panel. (Such action auto-commit adjustment and choose the layer.)
- Tap outside your canvas area in the document window.
- Tap the external area of the bounding box in your canvas area.
- Tap 'Enter (Windows)' or 'Return (Mac OS)', tap the 'Commit' button in your options bar, or double-tap inside the transformation marquee.
- For you to stop the transformation, tap 'Esc' or tap the 'Cancel' button in your bar options.

Note:

When transforming a bitmap photo (vs. a path or shape), the photo becomes somehow less sharp every time you carry out a transformation; thus doing various commands before you apply the increasing transformation is better to applying every transformation differently.

CHAPTER FOUR

PHOTOSHOP KEYBOARD SHORTCUTS AND PHOTOSHOP TOOLS: GENERAL TIPS AND SHORTCUTS

Keyboard shortcuts can be used effectively when using Adobe Photoshop. The keyboard shortcuts can be customized in Photoshop on your desktop.

You can summarize, view and edit keyboard shortcuts in your Keyboard Shortcuts dialog box. To see this in the Photoshop, choose 'Edit' then 'Keyboard Shortcuts' or use the keyboard shortcuts below:

- Alt + Shift + Control + K (Windows)
- Alt + Shift + Command + K (macOS)

On newer MacBook Pro models, the Touch Bar substitutes the function keys on above the keyboard. See this Apple documentation article to know how the use of function keys on these models.

Zoom in – Ctrl/Command +

Zoom Out – Ctrl/Command –

Pen Around – Hold down the space bar

Fit to Screen – 'Command/Ctrl + 0'

Hand Tool – Go round the image when zoomed in - Hold the spacebar

Rotate an Image - Tap the letter "R" on the keyboard, then tap and drag the mouse

Rotate in 15 degree increments – Ensure your rotate tool (R) is chosen + hold shift and drag the mouse

Below are some vital shortcuts to take note of:

1) Control + Alt + i (Command + Option + i) = Adjust the image size.

2) Control + Alt + c (Command + Option + c) = Adjust canvas size.

3) Control + + (Command + +) = Zoom in.

4) Control + - (Command + -) = Zoom out.

5) Control + ' (Command + ') = Display or conceal the grid, the automatically-generated vertical and horizontal lines that aids the alignment of objects to the canvas.

Choosing your Right Tools

These shortcuts will trigger different forms of tools, such as "Brush," "Lasso," or even "Spot Healing Brush." Among these tools, though, they have various functions. Under the "Magic Wand" tool group, for instance, you have the choice of executing a new selection or include and subtract from an existing one.

Each of these tools has a shortcut on your keyboard, and some of them have been outlined below:

5) Pointer, a.k.a. Move Toolpointer-tool.png

6) **Move Tool** – Enables you to change the position of an image or the layer round. It controls or commands 'T' to free transform and resize or rotate the layer and press 'enter' to confirm or it can as well be used to move pixels.

7) **Magic Wand Tool** – It creates selection around a consistently colored area.

8) **Rectangular Marquee Tool** – Creates rectangular selection or squares if you hold down the shift key

9) **Elliptical Marquee Tools** – It creates elliptical selections or circles if you hold down the shift key

10) **Lasso Tool** – It creates a custom freehand selection

11) **Polygonal lasso tool** – It creates straight edge selections

11) **Quick Selection tool** – It works just like a brush that paints selections by finding and following edges

12) **Brush tool** – It is amongst the most used tool that paints the layer with the foreground color you choose by clicking this box Note: The size and level of hardness can be adjusted to achieve different

outcomes. You can also change the brush tip or download your own for more creative results.

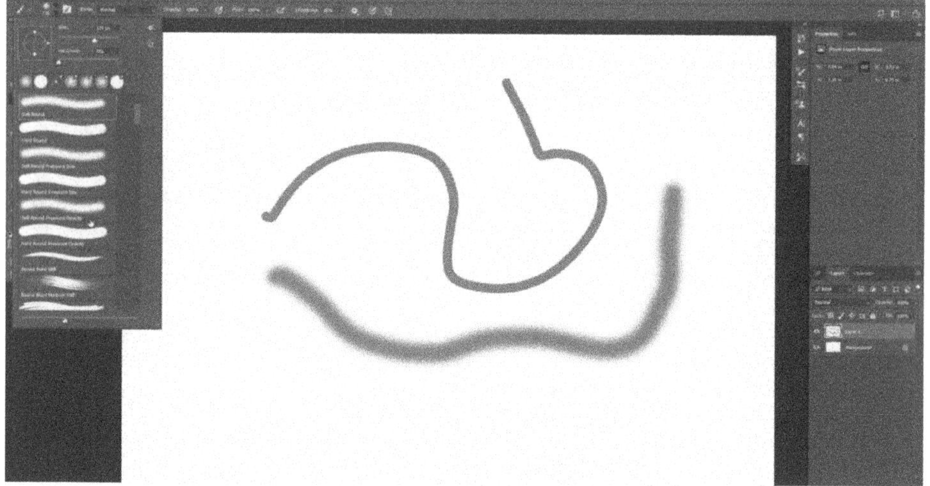

13) **The Clone Stamp Tool** – It samples a point from an area. Hold to option and click once to sample and then paints it on another area

14) **The Type Tool** T– Allows you to add and edit text

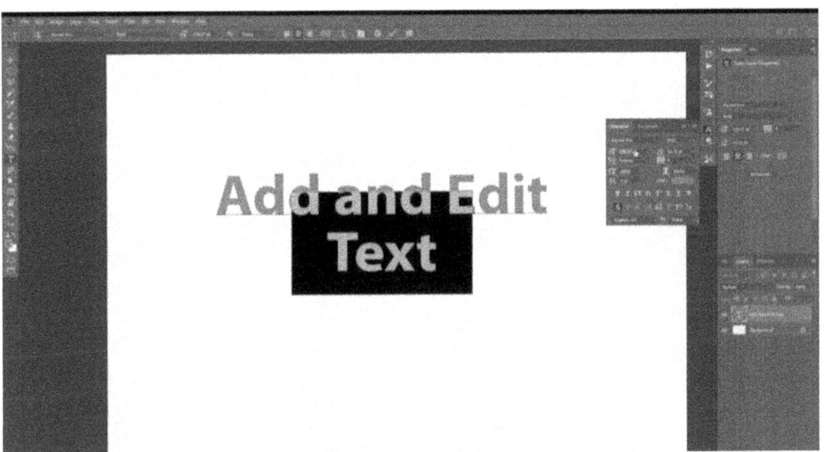

15) **The Pen Tool** – This is another highly important Photoshop tool that is used to create custom paths that can be later converted to selections by Ctrl + Command and Enter or shapes.

16) **The Rectangle, Ellipse, Polygon, Line and Custom Shape tool** - It allows you to create vector shapes that have a bunch of settings like fill color, stroke color and thickness.

Add and Edit
Text

Add and Edit
Text

CHAPTER FIVE

ADOBE COLOR PICKER OVERVIEW

In your Adobe Color Picker, you select colors with four color models: RGB, HSB, CMYK and Lab. The Adobe Color Picker can be used to set the foreground color, text color and background color. Target colors can also be set for various commands, options and tools.

The Adobe Color Picker can be configured to enable you to select just the color that is a portion of the web-safe palette or select from particular color systems.

The Adobe Color Picker can be configured to allow you choose only colors that are portion of the web-safe palette or choose from specific color systems. You can also get an HDR (high dynamic range) picker to select colors to be used in HDR images.

Note: If you select a color in the Adobe Color Picker, it at once shows the numeric values for Lab, RGB, CMYK, HSB, and hexadecimal numbers which are suitable for showing how the various color models explain a color.

Though by default Photoshop uses the Adobe Color Picker, you can as well use another color picker different from the Adobe Color Picker when you set a preference.

For instance, you can make use of the in-built color picker of your computer's functioning system or a third-party plug-in color picker.

Show the Color Picker

- In your toolbox, tap the background or foreground color selection box.
- In your Color panel, tap the 'Set Background Color' or 'Set Foreground Color' selection box.
- The Color Picker can also be accessible while features allow you to select a color. For instance, by tapping the color switch in your bar options for some tools, or the eye droppers in several color adjustment dialog boxes.

Select a color using the Adobe Color Picker

- You can choose a color when you enter color combination values in RGB, HSB and Lab text boxes or simply using the color field and the color slider.

- To choose a color with the color field or color slider, tap the color slider or take the color slider triangle to configure a color combination. Then change the position of the round marker or tap in the color field. This configures the other double color combinations.
- As you change the color with the color slider and color field, the numeric values for the various color models change accordingly. The rectangle at the right side of the color slider shows the new color at the upper half and the unique color at the bottom.

Note: You can choose a color at the external part of the Adobe Color Picker window and when you move your pointer over the image, the window adjusts it to an Eyedropper tool. You can now choose a color by tapping the image. The chosen color is shown in the Adobe Color Picker. You can take the Eyedropper tool to anywhere on the desktop by tapping in the image and pressing down the mouse button. You can select a color when you leave the mouse button.

CHAPTER SIX

ABOUT PHOTOSHOP LAYER

Convert a background into a Photoshop layer

- Double-click Background in the Layers panel, or choose Layer then New and Layer from Background.
- Set layer options. (See Create layers and groups.)
- Click 'OK.'

Convert a Photoshop layer into a background

- Select a Photoshop layer in the Layers panel.
- Choose Layer then 'New' then 'Background From Layer.'
- Any transparent pixels in the layer are converted to the background color, and the layer drops to the bottom of the layer stack.

Note: You cannot form a background by giving a regular layer the title, Background—you need to use the Background from Layer command.

Duplicate Photoshop layers

Layers can be duplicated inside an image or into something different or even a new image

How to duplicate a Photoshop layer or group inside an image

- Choose a group or a layer in the Layers panel and do any of the following:
- Drag the group or layer to make a New Layer button
- Select 'Duplicate Layer' or 'Duplicate Group' from your Layers menu or the Layers panel menu. Use a title for the group or layer, and tap 'OK.'

How to duplicate a Photoshop layer or group into another image entirely

- Launch the source and images destination.
- From your Layers panel of the image source, choose one or additional layers or a layer group and do any of the following:

- Take the group from your layers or layers panel to the image destination
- Choose the 'Move' tool, and drag from the image source to the image destination. The layer or duplicated group would display on top of the active layer in your Layers panel of the image destination.
- Shift-drag to take the content image to a similar location it occupies in the image source (when the image destination and the image source have similar pixel dimensions) or the middle of the document window (when the image destination and source have separate pixel dimensions).
- Select 'Duplicate Layer' or 'Duplicate Group' from your Layers panel menu or Layers menu. Select the document destination from the Document displayed menu, and tap 'OK.'
- Click 'Select' then 'All to choose all pixels on the layer' and select 'Edit' then 'Copy'.

- Then select 'Edit' then 'Paste' in the image destination. (This technique copies only the pixels without layer properties like blending mode.)

Make a new document from your Photoshop layer or group

- Select a layer or a group from your Layers panel
- Select 'Duplicate Layer' or 'Duplicate Group' from Layers menu or your Layers panel menu.
- Select 'New' from the Document displayed menu, and tap 'OK.'

Sample from all visible Photoshop layers

The original performance of the Magic Wand, Mixer Brush, Smudge, Sharpen, Blur, Clone Stamp, Paint Bucket, and Healing Brush tools is to display color just from pixels on your active layer. Meaning that you can sample or smudge in one layer.

- To sample or smudge pixels from every layer visible with these tools, choose 'Sample All Layers' from your options bar.
- Adjust transparency preferences

- In the Windows, select 'Edit' then 'Preferences' and 'Transparency & Gamut'; in Mac OS, select 'Photoshop' then 'Preferences' and 'Transparency & Gamut'.
- Select a color and size for the transparency checkerboard, or select 'None' for Grid Size to conceal the transparency checkerboard.
- Tap 'OK.'

CHAPTER SEVEN

HOW TO CUT OUT IN PHOTOSHOP

The following techniques revealed here are select and mask and Quick select that is good for things such as fur and hair. You will also see a color range which is remarkable for things such as trees.

Cut Out Hair in Photoshop

For this first method that works on only Photoshop CC, we will begin with an image of a woman having red hair. The hair is curly, therefore, would be somehow more difficult than straight hair. This method also works on fur.

- Open up the layer's point

- Duplicate the background layer by pressing 'Command + J
- Rename the duplicate background layer
- Go to the eraser tool and select 'Background Eraser Tool'

Note: The hardness and size of your eraser brush can be adjusted in the dropdown menu Take the quick selection tool from your toolbox.

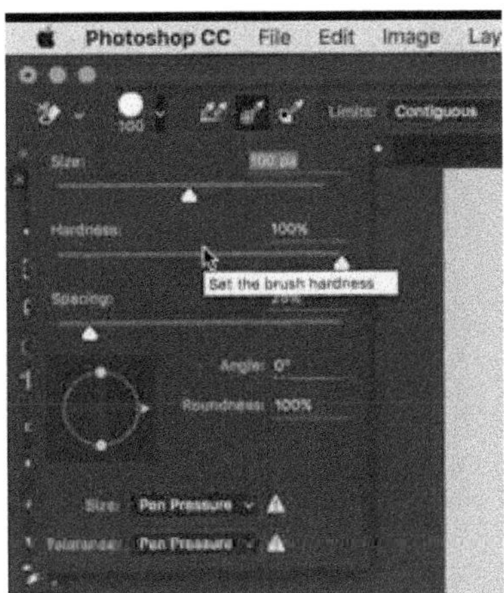

- There are also other few options to cut out hair effectively by resampling once
- The limit can as well be set to 'Discontinuous' and adjust the tolerance level

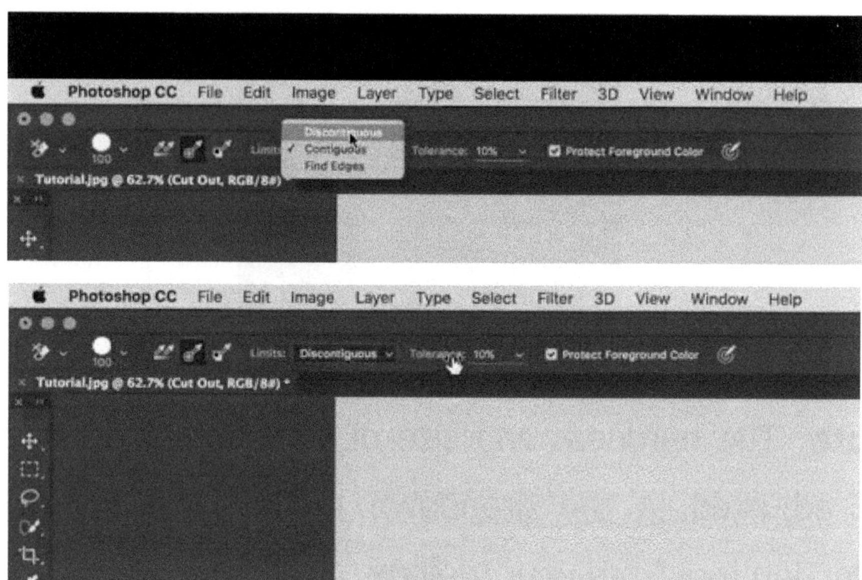

- To increase the brush size and start working with a 10% tolerance, this is the effect that would be gotten

- And if you zoom – in, you would notice that the result is not accurate.

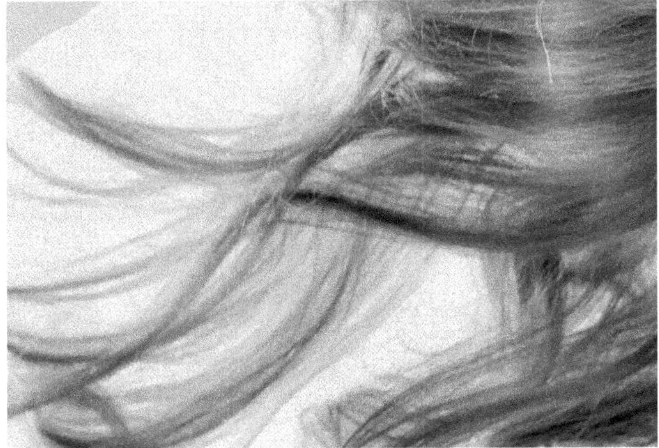

- You can then select 'Protect foreground color' to sample some of the hair using a brownie orange color

- As soon as you've got all the options set, e.g. your brush should be 50% hard just left click on the path of the background

- When you do the same in an environment where there's no hair and closer to the skin, it cuts into the face of the image which means that it has to be done manually.

- Select your eraser tool and bring your brush size down and start painting because if the brush size is too big, you would get something faded. So when working on something detailed, always ensure to bring your brush size down and zoom-in a lot closer

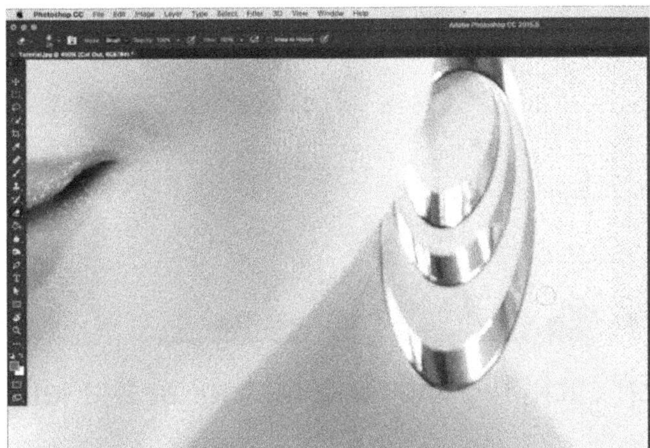

- When you're done, zoom it in and create another layer by tapping on the create new layer icon

- Then drag it under the layer you've named

- Select any color like the vibrant orange

- Then click 'fill' with the fill tool at the left side

- Select the cut out layer (that is, already named layer) and select the eraser tool again to enable you paint the places where the background eraser tool have not taken all background out but has taken some

- You can also turn your background to a plain white background by clicking Command + U to popup the Hue/Saturation dialogue box

- Drag the lightness to the end right

CUT OUT TREES WITH COLOR RANGE (APPLICABLE IN ALL PHOTOSHOP VERSIONS).

In this lesson, we will learn how to cut out trees with color Range. This tool is also good to cut out transparency, such as liquid and glass smoke.

This technique is good for selections and when the focus is difficult with enough holes, but an even color behind it.

Step 1: Use Color Range to Create a Selection in Photoshop

- Click 'Select' then 'Color Range.'
- A dialog box would pop-up

Step 2

- Select the left 'Eyedropper' tool.
- Tap the background, select the colors that are very common and next to the subject. The areas selected would display a bit of white.

Step 3: Refining the Selection

- Tap on the eyedropper having a + close to it.
- Drag it through the background to include it in the selection.

- If you notice you're missing some part, click again on the white area, view the preview window and notice there is white and black; and it's the main objective to get closer to this.

Step 4

- Slide the hairiness slider to improve the selection and catch the focus nice and black while the background would be white.
- Tap 'ok.'
- Observe the marching ants segment. The background has been successfully selected.

Step 5: Masking the Selection

- Let's cut out the selection: Since the background has been selected, we intend to upturn cut out area. (Hide the background and Display the subject). Due to this, we will tap down the 'Alt/Option' key and tap the new Layer mask. (Once the subject is choosen, then don't hold down 'Alt/Option'). Tap the Layer Mask icon.
- You will notice that a layer mask has been formed.

Using the Pen Tool in Photoshop to Cut Out Selections of

Hard Edged

In clean edges, the pen tool is better. It resolves to the better choice for easier shapes needing a crisp edge. Though it's among the toughest tools in Photoshop to get used to, when you get it, you'll find it very useful.

Step 1: Make a Rough Edge with the Pen Tool

- There's an easier way to use a pen tool that works pretty quickly, it'll be introduced to you here.
- Select the pen tool from your toolbar. Ensure the options above show the path and not a shape.
- Tap on the side where you wish to start and drag in the way that you wish to create your path
- Select the initial curve in the object and tap and drag once more. At this moment, you'll see a flexible line amid the two points. Check closely how it will adjust while you drag near or additionally away from the point, otherwise what occurs when the direction is changed. Don't panic

about precision at this point, because all we intend to achieve this is to create a path that roughly follows the outline of the shape.

- To stop drawing the path, take your cursor through the actual first point. While you hover, you will observe a small circle, tap on the point to finish the drawing and close the path.

Tip: The objective is to plan your subject with the minimum amount of possible points.

Step 2: Refine the Path

Several persons have attempted to get a perfect path the main time, though it's ok but I would prefer to split it into two stages.

- Below the Path Selection tool, choose the 'Direct Selection' tool.
- Then you can tap on the point to stimulate it.
- Zoom in well and near and cautiously drag the points into location. Tap the ends of the handles to adjust the angle of the curves.
- Pull and push the end points to adjust the curve's steepness. You may find it awkward at the initial

stage but constant practice will make it easier to understand.

Tip: To change one side of the curve, press down 'Alt/Option' as you drag to an endpoint.

Step 3: Add Points to the Curve

- If you drag a point to a fitted area with many curves, it will look complicated at first.
- Select your pen tool with the + on it to include a point.
- Tap and free on the track, where you wish to include additional anchor point
- You will then find a new point.
- You can choose to head back to your straight selection tool to continue using the + pen tool (their function is similar when dragging points)
- Take the new point to the right position and now you have a fine curve.
- End the refining path with the methods displayed.

Step 4: Concluding the Path

- When you are through, we should consider taking the external points to entirely cover the sky.

- Drag the side points

Step 5: Creating a Selection from a Path

- Head to the Paths panel
- You will observe the path as "Work Path." This path can be saved and used as a clipping group in QuarkXpress or InDesign. (When you are heading to a layout app for print, it is a better option due to the path being a vector that prints and sells better than pixels). For compositing work on Photoshop, change to a mask and selection in the following steps.
- In this situation, we would turn it to a selection. Press down Cmd/Ctrl and tap the work path in your Paths panel.
- You would then see a marching ant section
- Press down 'Alt/Option' to make an inverted mask.
- Now, we have a good cutout with smooth edges as seen.

CHAPTER EIGHT

ADOBE PHOTOSHOP SELECTION TOOLS

Adobe gives several tools for selection: Quick Mask, Elliptical Marquee, Rectangular Marquee, Magnetic Lasso, Polygonal Lasso, and Magic Wand.

The use of Quick Mask Mode is the most effective way of making a quick selection in Adobe Photoshop.

Quick Mask mode

- To change from Standard method to Quick Mask method, tap the button Quick Mask mode below the part of your Toolbox or use the hotkey Q.
- Paint through the places to be selected using a hard edge Brush (areas selected in Quick Mask mode are usually highlighted in a semi-transparent red)
- Then go back to the Standard mode by tapping the button 'Standard mode' below the Toolbox and invert the selection with the Command Select and Inverse. It is difficult when inverting the

selection in the Quick Mask mode, that is, the unpainted areas that are part of this selection.

Note: If you set chosen areas in the Options of Quick Mask (opened when you double click on the 'Quick Mask' button), the selection does not need to be inverted, and also you can change the highlighted color and the opacity here.

Tips on the Options of Quick Mask Options:

- Open the Options when you double click on the Quick Mask button.
- When the masked areas option is active, the non-marked areas with red will be chosen.
- When the selected area option is active, the marked areas with red will be chosen.

The Elliptical marquee and Rectangular marquee tools

The Elliptical marquee and Rectangular marquee tools are concealed in the Toolbox below one and the similar icon. The icon on the Toolbox shows the last tool being used. To launch the floating menu right-click on an arrow below the right corner of the icon displaying.

Elliptical marquee: The Elliptical marquee tool choses circles and ellipses.

To choose an elliptical area, do the following:

Step 1: Choose the 'Elliptical marquee' tool from your Toolbox by tapping on the icon. The 'Elliptical marquee' tool, or (But if the 'Elliptical marquee' wasn't the previous tool used) choose it from the fluctuating window.

Step 2: Take your mouse cursor to the point where the image is located at the corner of an imagined rectangle using an inscribed ellipse should be, and tap the left button.

Step 3: Press and hold the left button, take your cursor diagonally to an opposite corner and free the button.

- To choose an area with a circle in the image, create a selection while holding down your 'Shift' key. Keep in mind that if you have an area selected, the new selection will be included in the former one. To dodge this, you should tap your 'Shift' key only while you begin selecting a new area.

Rectangular marquee: The Rectangular marquee tool selects all square and rectangular areas. To choose a rectangular area, do the following:

Step 1: The Rectangular marquee tool can be activated when you click on the icon, or (in case the 'Rectangular marquee' tool was not the previous tool used) choose it from the moving window.

Step 2: Take your mouse cursor to the image point where the side of an imagined rectangle ought to be, and tap the left side of your mouse button.

Step 3: Pressing and Holding the left button diagonally take your cursor to the opposite side and free the button.

- In choosing a square area of an image, make your selection by pressing down your Shift key.
- To select a square area of the image make a selection keeping the Shift key pressed. Keep in mind that if you have an area selected before the new selection will be included in the former one. Tap your 'Shift' key only to avoid this when you begin to choose a new area.

The Lasso, Magnetic Lasso and Polygonal Lasso tools

The Lasso, Magnetic Lasso and Polygonal Lasso tools are concealed in the Toolbox below one and the similar icon. The icon on your Toolbox shows the previous tool selected. To launch the floating menu right-click on an arrow below the right side of the icon displayed.

Lasso

The Lasso tool enables the creation of freehand selections.

To make a freehand selection you should:

Step 1: Choose the Lasso tool from your Toolbox when you left-click on the icon 'Lasso tool', or (if you discover that Lasso tool was not the previous tool used) choose it from your floating window.

Step 2: Take the mouse cursor to an object that you must choose and outline it while leaving your left button tapped.

Magnetic Lasso

The Magnetic Lasso tool creates a freehand selection.

If you choose to use the Magnetic Lasso tool, you do not necessarily have to follow accurately the contour of an object. If an object is standing out in contrast to the background, the border of the areas selected will be automatically outlined when you take your cursor along an object.

To use the Magnetic lasso tool in selecting an area:

Step 1: Choose the 'Magnetic Lasso' tool from your Toolbox by tapping on the 'Magnetic Lasso' tool icon, or (in case Magnetic Lasso wasn't the previous tool used) take it from your floating window.

Step 2: Take your mouse cursor to the edge of the object that you want to select.

Step 3: Tap the button at the left and begin to drag your cursor through the object. Take note of fastening points displaying as you outline the object and if you make a click. If a fastening point is not relevant, it can be removed when you press the 'Delete' key and go back to the former fastening point to keep outlining your object.

Step 4: Close the contour that is linked to the main fastening point with the previous one by taking your cursor to the main point or by double-clicking.

Polygonal Lasso tool

The Polygonal lasso tool creates freehand selections, but the contour is made up of conventional segments. Do the following to create a selection:

Step 1: Choose the 'Polygonal Lasso' tool from your Toolbox by tapping on the Polygonal Lasso tool icon, or (in case the Polygonal Lasso was not the previous tool used) choose it from your floating window.

Step 2: Take your cursor to wherever point close to the object to be selected and tap your left mouse button - it'll automatically be your first point of the contour.

Step 3: Take your cursor to the subsequent point of the contour, not distancing it from the previous one and left-click on it once more. Automatically, the program will draw a straight line within the two points.

Step 4: Continue putting points in this mode until the entire object is selected before you can close the contour.

Magic Wand

The Magic Wand tool outlines a constantly colored area. You can configure Tolerance in the palette Options of your Magic Wand tool. The more the value, the higher colors will fall into the areas selected. The Tolerance value varies from 0 – 255. By Tolerance equivalent to 0, the areas selected will be only represented by a single color, by Tolerance equivalent to 255, every color of an image will be chosen, that is the entire image.

To choose a constantly colored area, do the following:

Step 1: Choose the 'Magic Wand' tool in your Toolbox by tapping the 'Magic Wand' tool icon.

Step 2: Take your cursor to the pixel of an image that must be added to selection and left-click on it. Therefore, an outline would display around the pixel. It adds colors of the image like the color of the chosen pixel due to the definite Tolerance value.

The selection tools are effective because of the elasticity of their usage; you can choose to add or subtract, or even intersect a particular selection.

To include an area to the former selection you can tap the 'Shift' key before using a selection tool and, continue holding it, create a new selection.

In subtracting an area from the former selection, you can tap the Alt key (Option in Mac) before using a selection tool and continue holding it, creating a new selection.

Photoshop color picker

In Photoshop, you can regulate the white balance for jpeg in two separate ways. Technique one is to choose image adjustments and color balance. The sliders can be viewed for separate color classifications that can be used in adjusting the color cast of an image. Also, curves can be adjusted by choosing image then adjustment and curves. Tap the white dropper and tap an area of your image that's supposed to be white (or tap the center dropper and choose a neutral grey), then you will see the changes.

Dimensions of colors

In the past, a lot of researchers have put into consideration to sort colors considering the color theory in a way that would enhance their notation and describing characteristics.

Each color has three (3) dimensions namely: hue, lightness and saturation usually referred to as the HSL method, used in Photoshop and ought to be the nearest to anything the human eye can view.

Hue

Clear colors in its complete strength are specified by their hue that adjusts as we go through the color circle. Hue is a feature through which one color is differentiated from another: orange from yellow, yellow from green, green from blue etc. Colors that are contrary in the color wheel are balancing colors.

Lightness

Color brightness or lightness is the next color dimension. Two colors can be of a similar shade but separate color lightness. Due to their lightness, we can differentiate light blue from dark blue, light red from dark red etc. Colors from the color range have their normal grade of lightness once they are very wet. Concentrated yellow for instance is the brightest, whereas purple is the darkest color in a color circle.

The brightness grade can be adjusted by including a darker or brighter color to it. Ideally, while including white to a light saturated yellow, what adjusts is the level of brightness. But basically, it's not possible to isolate brightness; when you mix yellow with white color, it makes it brighter but less saturated. By including black or white to a color, it changes its shade. Including red to black will make it look cooler, including yellow to black will make it appear greenish.

Saturation

When the color in an image is muted or appears dull, the level of saturation can be increased to make them appear brighter.

Then again, the level of saturation can be reduced to enable the color less bright. If the saturation is completely removed, it will result in a black-and-white, or grayscale image.

To change saturation, include a Hue/Saturation adjustment layer. Then tap and drag the Saturation slider in your properties panel to reduce or increase the saturation.

Note: If the saturation is too much, it results in the image losing its details and for better, it is recommended to use 'Chrome web browser' with these interactive features.

Converting to black and white

As mentioned earlier, when you completely remove the saturation by configuring it to -100, it will make a black and white image. Nevertheless, this technique does not offer you enough control over how the black and white version will appear. For best outcomes, you can make a Black and White adjustment layer.

Since black and white images do not have colors, the tones (i.e. the various shades gray) are particularly important. A Black and White alteration layer enables you to regulate how the various colors are mixed to make a particular tone that can make a vital dissimilarity on how the finishing image appears.

CHAPTER NINE

HOW TO USE PHOTOSHOP FILTERS

Step 1

Firstly, ensure the image is not too large. The larger the image, the lengthier it will take for Photoshop to apply the filter. In resizing an image to a size more suitable for testing, Head to image the image size and adjust the values.

Step 2

The next step is to change the image to a 'Smart Object.' It will enable you to change or even eliminate the effect of a filter not touching the original image. To perform this, right-click the layer and choose "Convert to Smart Object."

Step 3

Let's begin with something simpler. Go to 'Filter' then 'Oil Paint.' On your right, you can see settings that will enable you to turn the image to an oil painting. Test with your sliders to view how they would affect the image and how you can make a natural outcome with them. In the situation of extreme filters such as this one, it’s best to use a subtle effect that would not obviously appear digital.

Once you're through, tap ‘OK.’ The outcome will be used on the photo, but due to Smart Object, you can simply turn it off to view the original photo.

Step 4

Not every filter can be used for such dramatic effect. At times, you may want to create a slight correction. A sharpening filter would be ideal. Head into ‘Filter’, then ‘Sharpen’ and ‘Smart Sharpen.’ At this point, you can make the sharpening very correct, even if you require a subtle or an additional artistic effect.

Step 5

You may as well wish to do it another way and blur the photo, without leaving many details. There’s also a filter for this, Head into ‘Filter’ tap ‘Blur’ then ‘Smart Blur.’ This particular filter does not blur the whole image, but tries to blur the specific areas that are wisely detected. The end result can be changed according to the way you like it with the sliders.

Step 6

Photographers always wish to dodge noise in photos, but it's sometimes needed for a creative effect. That is the reason Photoshop has a distinct filter to make this possible. Head into 'Filter' click 'Noise' then 'Add Noise' and drag your slider to include some less for further visible grain. By doing this, you can simply include some character of an old photo to your image.

Step 7

Photoshop can as well adjust lighting in your photo to an extent. Head into 'Filter' click 'Render' then 'Lighting Effects.' Such a tool enables you to include an illusion of a different light source, to conceal some places in the shadow and show others through contrast. It might take few practice to make a convincing effect using this tool, but it can be used as a powerful tool if you can understand it. For instance, it can be used in creating a vignette effect.

Step 8

Not every filter can be used on the 'Smart Objects', therefore, lets convert the layer to a recent one of them (right-click then Rasterize). Head into 'Filter' then click 'Blur' and 'Iris Blur.' This is a very difficult filter giving you enough space for customization to make the precise effect you require. It can be used in simulating depth of a field or to bring attention to a particular area through blurring the rest.

Step 9

Photoshop as well has an entire library of distinct effects for images. Head into 'Filter' then 'Filter Gallery.' Zoom it out to view the whole image. On your right, you have various filters grouped into different kinds. Let's take a look at a few of them.

Dry Brush, for instance, can convert a photo to smooth painting. You can get a simple but a sophisticated result. This filter can as well be useful if you wish to clear an image that is blur, to change its lack of element into a feature instead of a flaw. If you wish to view what has been adjusted, tap the eye icon below the filter.

Step 10

The Watercolor filter ideally has a related goal, but the result is extremely not the same. It includes certain subtle texture and darkens the previously dark areas, including an attractive contrast. It may not necessarily appear like a watercolor painting, but it's also a very stimulating effect.

Step 11

Most filters in your Filter Gallery convert your image in a drawing or a painting, and though each offers their distinctive effects, they are all alike in this regard. Therefore, let's see one of these which work in a separate way – Halftone Pattern. It uses a color based on your background and foreground color, therefore, if you need a wise artistic effect, you can use them for experiment as well.

Step 12

Lastly, there's a trick that enables you to apply all these filters and others in a different way leading to exceptional results. Go to 'Channels' and choose any of the layers instead of RGB.

Step 13

Keep everything visible.

CONCLUSION

The functions of Adobe Photoshop can be awesome to use for a lot of beginners especially the photographers. Therefore this detailed guideline has been put together and covers the basics of the common and unarguably the most powerful processing tool on the market.

A lot of us have heard people saying something similar to this "This image is photoshopped" at least once. Even the non-photographers use this slogan at all times while talking about images that are digitally-manipulated. Which means, Photoshop is now the same with post processing?

Despite there being a lot of tools used in processing an image, very few can be compared to Photoshop in terms of functionality and features. Without any doubt, Photoshop is a massive and multifaceted software piece, and there are a lot of built-in and third party tools accessible for it.

The nature of always learning in Photoshop calls for a steep learning curve. There isn't anyone that can say "I understand everything in Photoshop". Rather than saying that, try to study everything that concerns the software, a lot of us choose to learn the specific tools that we really require on a daily basis.

As soon as you study a specific tool in Photoshop, it might take time and constant practice to put it into good use. It might even be a slow procedure, but if you can get used to it, the outcomes are extremely worthwhile.

ABOUT THE AUTHOR

Michael A. Palmer is a professional writer, a digital photo editor including a photographer. He technically edits for entertainment weekly in America. He has authored various digital imaging books as well as Beginner's Guide to Color Correction and Enhancement with Adobe Photoshop, Special Effect, and Step by Step Photography. He currently resides in Los Angeles, California.

He is a father of three and enthusiastic about what he does. He over the years spent time in achieving his goals and will not stop until he is satisfied.

www.ingramcontent.com/pod-product-compliance
Ingram Content Group UK Ltd.
Pitfield, Milton Keynes, MK11 3LW, UK
UKHW022017190726
13853UKWH00005B/1981

9 798506 736899